AMAZING INVENTORS & INNOVATORS

# GEORGE EASTMAN

**LYNN DAVIS**

**Consulting Editor, Diane Craig, M.A./Reading Specialist**

**Super Sandcastle**

An Imprint of Abdo Publishing
abdopublishing.com

abdopublishing.com

Published by Abdo Publishing, a division of ABDO, PO Box 398166, Minneapolis, Minnesota 55439. Copyright © 2016 by Abdo Consulting Group, Inc. International copyrights reserved in all countries. No part of this book may be reproduced in any form without written permission from the publisher. Super SandCastle™ is a trademark and logo of Abdo Publishing.

Printed in the United States of America, North Mankato, Minnesota
062015
092015

Editor: Liz Salzmann
Content Developer: Nancy Tuminelly
Cover and Interior Design and Production: Mighty Media, Inc.
Photo Credits: Library of Congress, Shutterstock, Wikicommons

Library of Congress Cataloging-in-Publication Data

Davis, Lynn, 1981- author.
George Eastman / Lynn Davis ; consulting editor, Diane Craig, M.A./Reading Specialist.
     pages cm. --  (Amazing inventors & innovators)

Audience: K to grade 4
ISBN 978-1-62403-722-1

1. Eastman, George, 1854-1932--Juvenile literature. 2.  Photographic industry--United States--Biography--Juvenile literature. 3.  Kodak camera--Juvenile literature. 4.  Inventors--United States--Biography--Juvenile literature.  I. Title.

TR140.E3D38 2016
770.92--dc23
[B]
                         2014046598

Super SandCastle™ books are created by a team of professional educators, reading specialists, and content developers around five essential components—phonemic awareness, phonics, vocabulary, text comprehension, and fluency—to assist young readers as they develop reading skills and strategies and increase their general knowledge. All books are written, reviewed, and leveled for guided reading, early reading intervention, and Accelerated Reader™ programs for use in shared, guided, and independent reading and writing activities to support a balanced approach to literacy instruction.

# CONTENTS

# GEORGE EASTMAN

Eastman and Thomas Edison, 1929

George Eastman was an American **innovator**. He made **film** that could be rolled up. He also made simple cameras. They were easy for anyone to use.

# GEORGE EASTMAN

**BORN:** July 12, 1854, Waterville, New York

**MARRIAGE:** never got married

**CHILDREN:** did not have any children

**DIED:** March 14, 1932, Rochester, New York

# EARLY LIFE

George Eastman grew up in New York. His father had a fruit farm. George went to school. He learned a lot on his own too.

Eastman's father, George Eastman Sr.

He had his first job when he was thirteen. He was an office boy. Later he became a bookkeeper.

Eastman as a teenager

Eastman as a young man

# VACATION PLANS

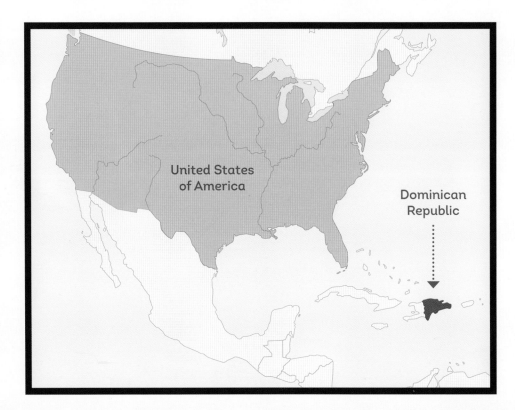

United States
of America

Dominican
Republic

George planned a vacation. He was going to the Dominican Republic. He wanted to **photograph** his trip.

He bought a camera. He took lessons to learn how to use it. But he never went on the trip.

# BIG AND BULKY

**Photography** gear was big and bulky. The camera had to sit on a **tripod**.

The pictures were on glass plates. Taking a picture needed a long **exposure**. Eastman wanted to make **photography** easier.

# FIGURING OUT FILM

Eastman figured out how to make **film**. He used paper. The paper had **chemicals** on it. The paper could be rolled up.

# He called the paper **film** Eastman American Film.

Roller holder for photographic film

# THE BIRTH OF KODAK

Next, Eastman made a camera. It was a box camera.

It came out in 1888. It used Eastman American **Film**.

## K IS FOR KODAK

George Eastman liked the letter *K*. He made up the name Kodak. It has two *K*s. He named his company the Eastman Kodak Company.

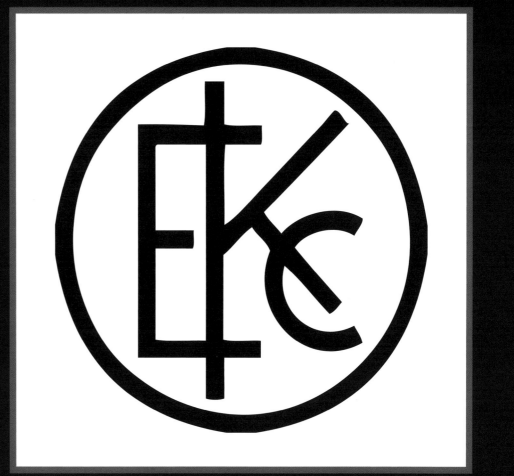

# ONE HUNDRED PHOTOS

The first Kodak cameras could take 100 pictures. Then the owner sent it to Kodak. Kodak printed the **photos**.

They put new **film** in the camera. Then they sent the camera and **photos** back to the owner.

These photos were taken
with a Kodak box camera.

# THE BROWNIE CAMERA

The Brownie camera came out in 1900. It was made for kids. It was very easy to use.

Kids and adults all enjoyed using Brownie cameras. Anyone could take **photos**!

Kodak made Brownie cameras for 70 years. There were 125 different models.

## WHAT'S IN A NAME?

The Brownie camera was named after cartoon characters created by Palmer Cox. They were very popular at the time. They were called Brownies.

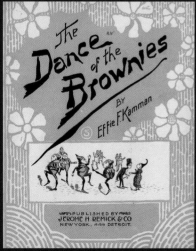

# PHOTOGRAPHY FOR THE PEOPLE!

George Eastman made **innovations** in **film**. He made innovations in cameras.

# He made **photography** easier than it had ever been before!

Belgian painter Henri Evenepoel used mirrors to take a selfie in 1898.

# MORE ABOUT EASTMAN

Eastman had a large ORGAN in his house. A man played the **organ** every morning for Eastman.

Eastman was very PRIVATE. He made a popular camera. But there are not many pictures of him.

Eastman HELPED CAUSES he believed in. He gave a lot of his money away.

# TEST YOUR KNOWLEDGE

1. What kind of farm did Eastman's father have?

2. Why did Eastman make up the name Kodak?

3. The Brownie camera was named after popular cartoon characters. True or false?

## THINK ABOUT IT!

What do you like to take pictures of?

ANSWERS: 1. Fruit farm 2. He liked the letter K 3. True

# GLOSSARY

**chemical** - something that reacts or changes when mixed with something else.

**exposure** - the amount of time light shines on film when taking a picture.

**film** - a thin material you can see through that is used for taking pictures.

**innovation** - a new way of doing something. Someone who does something in a new way is an innovator.

**organ** - a musical instrument with keys that push air through pipes.

**photograph** - 1. to make a picture using a camera. 2. a picture made using a camera. *Photo* is short for *photograph*.

**photography** - the art of taking pictures with a camera.

**tripod** - a stand with three legs.